D1014604

Presented to

By

On the Occasion of

Date

© 2009 by Barbour Publishing, Inc.

ISBN 978-1-60260-606-7

Text was compiled from the following: *365 Meditations for the Satisfied Soul, 365 Days of Joy, Prayers for Women, 365 Stress-Free Moments for Women, 365 Moments of Peace for Moms, Encouragement for Men, 365 Days of Love, 365 Ways to Wake Up Laughing,* and *Thinking of You,* published by Barbour Publishing, Inc.

Quotes without an attribution are unknown or anonymous authors.

Scripture quotations marked NLT are taken from the *Holy Bible,* New Living Translation, copyright © 1996. Used by permission of Tyndale House Publishers, Inc. Wheaton, Illinois 60189, U.S.A. All rights reserved.

Scripture quotations marked KJV are taken from the King James Version of the Bible.

Scripture quotations marked MSG are from *THE MESSAGE*. Copyright © by Eugene H. Peterson 1993, 1994, 1995, 1996, 2000, 2001, 2002. Used by permission of NavPress Publishing Group.

Scripture quotations marked NRSV are taken from the New Revised Standard Version Bible, copyright 1989, Division of Christian Education of the National Council of the Churches of Christ in the United States of America. Used by permission. All rights reserved.

Scripture quotations marked NIV are taken from the HOLY BIBLE, NEW INTERNATIONAL VERSION®. NIV®. Copyright © 1973, 1978, 1984 by International Bible Society. Used by permission of Zondervan. All rights reserved.

Scripture quotations marked NASB are taken from the New American Standard Bible, © 1960, 1962, 1963, 1968, 1971, 1972, 1973, 1975, 1977, 1995 by The Lockman Foundation. Used by permission.

Published by Barbour Publishing, Inc., P.O. Box 719, Uhrichsville, Ohio 44683, www.barbourbooks.com

Our mission is to publish and distribute inspirational products offering exceptional value and biblical encouragement to the masses.

Member of the
Evangelical Christian
Publishers Association

Printed in Indonesia.

WHISPERS OF
Joy

BARBOUR
PUBLISHING

God's Pattern

The patterns God plans
for our days are always changing
. . .rearranging. . .and each design
is unique. . .graced with His own
special beauty.

Joy in Living

Whether sixty or sixteen, there
is in every human being's heart
the love of wonder, the sweet
amazement at the stars and
starlike things, the undaunted
challenge of events, the unfailing
childlike appetite for what-next,
and the joy of the game of living.

SAMUEL ULLMAN

Daily Joys

Daily duties are daily joys,
because they are something
which God gives us to offer unto
Him, to do our very best,
in acknowledgment of His love.

EDWARD BOUVERIE PUSEY

My Delight

Send forth your light and your
truth, let them guide me; let them
bring me to your holy mountain,
to the place where you dwell. Then
will I go to the altar of God, to
God, my joy and my delight.

PSALM 43:3–4 NIV

Joy=Strength

[God] knows everything about us.
And He cares about everything.
Moreover, He can manage every
situation. And He loves us!
Surely this is enough to open the
wellsprings of joy. . . . And joy is
always a source of strength.

HANNAH WHITALL SMITH

Bliss

Only to sit and think of God,
Oh, what a joy it is!
To think the thought,
To breathe the Name:
Earth has no higher bliss.

FREDERICK W. FABER

Significance

Half the joy of life is in little things taken on the run. Let us run if we must—even the sands do that—but let us keep our hearts young and our eyes open that nothing worth our while shall escape us. And everything is worth its while if we only grasp it and its significance.

C. VICTOR CHERBULIEZ

All That Is Good

One who loves is borne on wings;
he runs, and is filled with joy; he is
free and unrestricted. He gives all
to receive all, and he has all in all;
for beyond all things he rests in
the one highest thing, from whom
streams all that is good.

THOMAS À KEMPIS

Under All Circumstances

We have a Father in heaven who is
almighty, who loves His children
as He loves His only begotten Son,
and whose very joy and delight it
is to. . .help them at all times and
under all circumstances.

GEORGE MÜLLER

Joyful Simplicities

Year by year the complexities of
this spinning world grow more
bewildering, and so each year
we need all the more to seek
peace and comfort in the joyful
simplicities.

God's Will

Always be joyful. Never stop
praying. Be thankful in all
circumstances, for this is God's
will for you who belong to Christ
Jesus.

1 THESSALONIANS 5:16–18 NLT

Watch God Work!

Cast your anxieties on the Lord.
Give them up! Let them go! Don't
let worries zap your strength and
your joy. Today is a gift from the
Lord. Don't sacrifice it to fears
and frustrations! Let them go. . .
and watch God work!

With Enthusiasm

To love God, to serve Him
because we love Him, is. . .our
highest happiness. . . . Love makes
all labor light. We serve with
enthusiasm where we love with
sincerity.

HANNAH MORE

World without End

Bring us, O Lord God. . .to enter
into that gate and dwell in that
house, where there shall be no
darkness nor dazzling, but one
equal light; no noise nor silence,
but one equal music. . .no ends nor
beginnings, but one equal eternity;
in the habitations of Thy majesty
and Thy glory, world without end.

JOHN DONNE

I Am Loved

I tell You my problems and You listen, Lord. I speak of the good things in my life and You smile. I ask You for advice, knowing it will come in Your time. I am no longer lonely; I am loved. Amen.

Live Such a Life

Be such a person, and live such a
life, that if every one were such as
you, and every life a life such as
yours, this earth would be God's
paradise.

PHILLIPS BROOKS

Praise You

O God, great and wonderful,
who has created the heavens,
dwelling in the light and beauty
of it; who has made the earth,
revealing Yourself in every flower
that opens; let not my eyes be
blind to You. . .teach me to praise
You, even as the lark which offers
her song at daybreak.

ISIDORE OF SEVILLE

Rubbing Elbows with Happiness

Sometimes our thoughts turn back
toward a corner in a forest,
or the end of a bank, or an orchard
powdered with flowers seen but
a single time. . .yet remaining in
our hearts and leaving in soul and
body an unappeased desire which
is not to be forgotten, a feeling
we have just rubbed elbows with
happiness.

GUY DE MAUPASSANT

Joy. . .in the Hands of God

Peace of conscience, liberty of
heart, the sweetness of abandoning
ourselves in the hands of God,
the joy of always seeing the light
grow in our hearts, finally, freedom
from the fears and insatiable
desires of the times, multiply a
hundredfold the happiness which
the true children of God possess.

FRANÇOIS FÉNELON

Great Delight

"The LORD your God is with you,
he is mighty to save. He will take
great delight in you, he will quiet
you with his love, he will rejoice
over you with singing."

ZEPHANIAH 3:17 NIV

Heights of Joy

Prayer is an upward leap of the heart, an untroubled glance toward heaven, a cry of gratitude and love which I utter from the depths of sorrow as well as from the heights of joy. It has supernatural grandeur that expands the soul and unites it with God.

THÉRÉSE OF LISIEUX

Sure Way to Happiness

If anyone would tell you the shortest, surest way to happiness and perfection, he must tell you to make it a rule to yourself to thank and praise God for everything that happens to you. For it is certain that whatever seeming calamity happens to you, if you thank and praise God for it, you turn it into a blessing.

WILLIAM LAW

A Sunbeam

Happiness is a sunbeam. . . .
When it strikes a kindred heart,
like the converged lights upon
a mirror, it reflects itself with
redoubled brightness. It is not
perfected until it is shared.

JANE PORTER

Be Alive To. . .

Life is what we are alive to.
It is not length but breadth. . . .
Be alive to. . .goodness, kindness,
purity, love, history, poetry, music,
flowers, stars, God, and eternal
hope.

MALTBIE D. BABCOCK

Your Success

If the day and night are such
that you greet them with joy,
and life emits a fragrance like
flowers and sweet-scented herbs,
is more elastic, more starry, more
immortal—that is your success.

HENRY DAVID THOREAU

Element of Joy

Into all our lives, in many
simple, familiar, homely ways,
God infuses this element of joy
from the surprises of life, which
unexpectedly brighten our days
and fill our eyes with light.

HENRY WADSWORTH LONGFELLOW

Be Glad

Be glad of life, because it gives you
the chance to love and to work and
to play and to look up at the stars
. . .and to spend as much time as
you can, with body and with spirit
in God's out-of-doors—these are
little guideposts on the footpath to
peace.

HENRY VAN DYKE

Bright with Hope

How could I be anything but quite
happy if I believed always that all
the past is forgiven, and all the
present furnished with power,
and all the future bright with hope.

JAMES SMETHAM

Shine!

Let the light of your face shine
upon us, O LORD. You have filled
my heart with greater joy than
when their grain and new wine
abound.

PSALM 4:6–7 NIV

Abundant Grace

The Lord's chief desire is to reveal Himself to you and, in order for Him to do that, He gives you the experience of enjoying His presence. He touches you, and His touch is so delightful that, more than ever, you are drawn inwardly to Him.

MADAME JEANNE GUYON

Made for Joy

Our hearts were made for joy.
Our hearts were made to enjoy
the One who created them. Too
deeply planted to be much affected
by the ups and downs of life,
this joy is a knowing and a being
known by our Creator. He sets our
hearts alight with radiant joy.

Endless Wonders

As we grow in our capacities to see
and enjoy the delights that God
has placed in our lives, life
becomes a glorious experience
of discovering His endless
wonders.

Belonging to Him

Our God is so wonderfully good
and lovely and blessed in every way
that the mere fact of belonging to
Him is enough for an untellable
fullness of joy!

HANNAH WHITALL SMITH

Happy Hearts

Our hearts are not made happy
by words alone. We should seek
a good and pure life, setting
our minds at rest and having
confidence before God.

THOMAS À KEMPIS

Watch the Joy Flow!

Want to know the secret of
walking in the fullness of joy?
Draw near to the Lord. Allow His
Spirit to fill you daily. Let Him
whisper sweet nothings in your ear
and woo you with His love.
The Spirit of God is your
Comforter, your Friend. He fills
you to overflowing. Watch the joy
flow!

Wonder of the World

I still find each day too short for
all the thoughts I want to think,
all the walks I want to take, all the
books I want to read, and all the
friends I want to see. The longer
I live, the more my mind dwells
upon the beauty and the wonder of
the world.

JOHN BURROUGHS

Huge Waves

Huge waves that would frighten an ordinary swimmer produce a tremendous thrill for the surfer who has ridden them. Let's apply that to our own circumstances. The things we try to avoid and fight against—tribulation, suffering, and persecution—are the very things that produce abundant joy in us.

OSWALD CHAMBERS

Nothing but Joy

My brothers and sisters,
whenever you face trials of any
kind, consider it nothing but joy,
because you know that the testing
of your faith produces endurance;
and let endurance have its full
effect, so that you may be mature
and complete, lacking in nothing.

JAMES 1:2–4 NRSV

The Tide Will Turn

When you get into a tight place and everything goes against you, 'til it seems as though you cannot hang on a minute longer, never give up then, for that is just the place and time that the tide will turn.

HARRIET BEECHER STOWE

Renewal

Should we feel at times
disheartened and discouraged,
a simple movement of heart toward
God will renew our powers. . . .
He will give us at the moment the
strength and courage that we need.

FRANÇOIS FÉNELON

Daily Blessings

The sun. . .in its full glory,
either at rising or setting—this,
and many other like blessings we
enjoy daily. . .because they are so
common, most men forget to pay
their praises. But let us not.

IZAAK WALTON

Beauty Is God's Handwriting

Never lose an opportunity
of seeing anything that is
beautiful; for beauty is God's
handwriting—a wayside
sacrament. Welcome it in every
fair face, in every fair sky, in every
fair flower, and thank God for it as
a cup of blessing.

RALPH WALDO EMERSON

Be Inspired

Take time in your day to be
inspired by something small—the
scent of a flower, a hug from a
child, an "I love you" from your
spouse. . . . Then thank God for
the little things in life.

Happiness and Yourself

Whether any particular day shall
bring to you more of happiness
or of suffering is largely beyond
your power to determine.
Whether each day of your life shall
give happiness or suffering rests
with yourself.

GEORGE S. MERRIAM

All I Need

O Father, You have draped me
in the garments of salvation and
wrapped me snugly in the robe of
righteousness. I am beautifully
adorned by You—for You.
You have given me all I need to
live a joyful life, and I rejoice in
Your gifts of beauty.

Moments

Occasionally in life there are
those moments of unutterable
fulfillment which cannot be
completely explained by those
symbols called words.
Their meanings can only be
articulated by the inaudible
language of the heart.

MARTIN LUTHER KING JR.

When You're Overwhelmed

Lord, I'm overwhelmed. . . . I often
lose sight of You. Please rejuvenate
my soul and help me look to You
for strength and comfort when
I need it most. Remind me that
I can't control everything and
that it's okay that I'm not perfect.
Amen.

Kind Words in Abundance

Kind words produce their own
image in men's souls; and a beautiful
image it is. They soothe and quiet
and comfort the hearer. . . .
We have not yet begun to use kind
words in such abundance as they
ought to be used.

BLAISE PASCAL

Showers of Blessing

We can hardly believe it when
God's more than enough provision
shines down upon us. What did we
do to deserve it? Nothing! During
such seasons, we can't forget to
thank Him for the many ways He
is moving in our lives. Our hearts
must overflow with gratitude to a
gracious and almighty God.

Into Joy

We pray that you'll have the
strength to stick it out over
the long haul—not the grim
strength of gritting your teeth
but the glory-strength God gives.
It is strength that endures the
unendurable and spills over
into joy.

COLOSSIANS 1:11 MSG

Inner Fire

In everyone's life, at some time,
our inner fire goes out. It is then
burst into flame by an encounter
with another human being.
We should all be thankful for
those people who rekindle the
inner spirit.

ALBERT SCHWEITZER

The Return

Instead of being unhappy, just let
your love grow as God wants it
to grow. Seek goodness in others.
Love more persons more. . .
unselfishly, without thought of
return. The return, never fear,
will take care of itself.

HENRY DRUMMOND

Blessing upon Blessing

Trust in the Redeemer's strength
. . .exercise what faith you have,
and by and by He shall rise upon
you with healing beneath His
wings. Go from faith to faith and
you shall receive blessing upon
blessing.

CHARLES H. SPURGEON

Think Pleasantly

I have resolved that from this day on, I will do all the business I can honestly, have all the fun I can reasonably, do all the good I can willingly, and save my digestion by thinking pleasantly.

ROBERT LOUIS STEVENSON

Full Bloom

I will sing for joy in GOD, explode
in praise from deep in my soul!
. . . For as the earth bursts with
spring wildflowers, and as a garden
cascades with blossoms, so the
Master, GOD, brings righteousness
into full bloom.

ISAIAH 61:10–11 MSG

Do Good!

Do all the good you can, by all the
means you can, in all the ways you
can, in all the places you can, at all
the times you can, to all the people
you can, as long as ever you can.

JOHN WESLEY

Do It Now

I expect to pass through life but
once. If, therefore, there can be
any kindness I can show, or any
good things I can do to any fellow
human being, let me do it now and
not defer it or neglect it, as I shall
not pass this way again.

WILLIAM PENN

Pass It On!

Have you had a kindness shown?
Pass it on; 'twas not given for thee
alone, pass it on; let it travel down
the years, let it wipe another's
tears, till in heaven the deed
appears, pass it on.

HENRY BURTON

Unfailing Love

Have you experienced God's
unfailing love? Then your
satisfaction is guaranteed.
He promises you'll never be left or
forsaken. Joy in Him will be your
portion for the rest of your life.

A New Song

God can make all things new in
our lives, just as His mercies greet
us in a new way every morning.
He can give us new life, a
new heart, new desires, a new
beginning, and a new song.

ROY LESSIN

Priceless!

This is the real gift: we have been given the breath of life, designed with a unique, one-of-a-kind soul that exists forever—whether we live it as a joy or with indifference doesn't change the fact that we've been given the gift of being now and forever. Priceless in value, we are handcrafted by God, who has a personal design and plan for each of us.

Renewed Joy

By reading the scriptures I am
so renewed that all nature seems
renewed around me and with
me. The sky seems to be a pure,
a cooler blue, the trees a deeper
green. The whole world is charged
with the glory of God, and I feel
fire and music under my feet.

THOMAS MERTON

The Heart's Gratitude

As flowers carry dewdrops,
trembling on the edges of the
petals, and ready to fall at the
first waft of the wind or brush of
bird, so the heart should carry its
beaded words of thanksgiving.
At the first breath of heavenly
flavor, let down the shower,
perfumed with the heart's
gratitude.

HENRY WARD BEECHER

Spare Moments

Guard well your spare moments.
They are like uncut diamonds.
Discard them and their value will
never be known. Improve them
and they will become the brightest
gems in a useful life.

RALPH WALDO EMERSON

Our Best Days Are Ahead

Change is never easy, particularly
when you have to let go of the
past. But oh, the joy of recognizing
that God sees into the future.
He knows that springtime is
coming. Our best days are ahead!

Wonderful Joy Ahead

So be truly glad. There is
wonderful joy ahead. . . .
You love him even though you
have never seen him. Though you
do not see him now, you trust him;
and you rejoice with a glorious,
inexpressible joy.

1 PETER 1:6, 8 NLT

New-Created

And if tonight my soul may find
her peace in sleep, and sink in
oblivion, and in the morning wake
like a new-opened flower, then I
have been dipped again in God,
and new-created.

D. H. LAWRENCE

Utterly Surrendered

It is wonderful what miracles God works in wills that are utterly surrendered to Him. He turns hard things into easy, and bitter things into sweet. It is not that He puts easy things in the place of the hard, but He actually changes the hard thing into an easy one.

HANNAH WHITALL SMITH

Joy-Giver

To be a joy-bearer and a joy-giver
says everything, for in our life,
if one is joyful, it means that one
is faithfully living for God, and
that nothing else counts; and if
one gives joy to others, one is
doing God's work.

JANET ERSKINE-STUART

Tomorrow...

Do not look forward to what
may happen tomorrow; the same
everlasting Father who cares for
you today will take care of you
tomorrow and every day. Either
He will shield you from suffering,
or He will give you unfailing
strength to bear it. Be at peace
then, and put aside all anxious
thoughts and imaginations.

ST. FRANCIS DE SALES

A Child's Heart

Dear Jesus, help me not be so busy
that I miss the small pleasures
You've sprinkled throughout my
day. . . . Give me a child's heart
that sees the lovely simple things
in life.

ELLYN SANNA

Never Underestimate. . .

Too often we underestimate the
power of a touch, a smile, a kind
word, a listening ear, an honest
compliment, or the smallest act
of caring, all of which have the
potential to turn a life around.

LEO BUSCAGLIA

A Good Haven to Sail For

To desire and strive to be of some service to the world, to aim at doing something which shall really increase the happiness and welfare and virtue of mankind—this is a choice which is possible for all of us; and surely it is a good haven to sail for.

HENRY VAN DYKE

Real Hope

Lord, You are my hope in an
often hopeless world. You are
my hope of heaven, my hope
of peace, my hope of change,
purpose, and unconditional love.
Fill the reservoir of my heart to
overflowing with the joy that real
hope brings. Amen.

Heavenly Environment

Cherish your visions; cherish your
ideals; cherish the music that
stirs your heart, the beauty that
forms in your mind, the loveliness
that drapes your purest thoughts,
for out of them will grow all
delightful conditions, all heavenly
environment.

JAMES ALLEN

Born to Eternal Life

O Divine Master, grant that I
may not so much seek. . .to be
understood as to understand; to be
loved as to love; for it is in giving
that we receive; it is in pardoning
that we are pardoned; and it is in
dying that we are born to eternal
life.

ST. FRANCIS OF ASSISI

My Heart Is Glad

I have set the LORD always
before me. Because he is at my
right hand, I will not be shaken.
Therefore my heart is glad and my
tongue rejoices; my body also will
rest secure.

PSALM 16:8–9 NIV

Sweetly and Tenderly

We are so preciously loved by God
that we cannot even comprehend
it. No created being can ever know
how much and how sweetly and
tenderly God loves them.

JULIAN OF NORWICH

Simple Charm

The splendor of the rose and the
whiteness of the lily do not rob
the little violet of its scent nor the
daisy of its simple charm. If every
tiny flower wanted to be a rose,
spring would lose its loveliness.

THÉRÈSE OF LISIEUX

Joy of Eternity

What will it be like to walk on
streets of gold, to see our loved
ones who have gone before us?
How thrilling to know we will one
day meet our Lord and Savior
face-to-face. He has gone to
prepare a place for us—and what a
place it will be!

Unchangeable Beauty

The beauty of the earth, the beauty of the sky, the order of the stars, the sun, the moon. . .their very loveliness is their confession of God: for who made these lovely mutable things, but He who is Himself unchangeable beauty?

ST. AUGUSTINE

Joy Mixed with Awe

The very act of planting a seed in
the earth has in it to me something
beautiful. I always do it with a joy
that is largely mixed with awe.

CELIA LAIGHTON THAXTER

Shouts of Joy

"For you will go out with joy,
and be led forth with peace;
the mountains and the hills will
break forth into shouts of joy
before you, and all the trees of the
field will clap their hands."

ISAIAH 55:12 NASB

Treasures of Nature

If we are children of God, we have
a tremendous treasure in nature
and will realize that it is holy and
sacred. We will see God reaching
out to us in every wind that blows,
every sunrise and sunset, every
cloud in the sky, every flower that
blooms, every leaf that fades.

OSWALD CHAMBERS

A Garden

To know someone here or there
with whom you feel there is an
understanding in spite of distances
or thoughts unexpressed—that
can make of this earth a garden.

JOHANN WOLFGANG VON GOETHE

All Things

All things bright and beautiful,
All creatures great and small,
All things wise and wonderful,
The Lord God made them all.

CECIL FRANCES ALEXANDER

Living Water

From God, great and small,
rich and poor, draw living water
from a living spring, and those
who serve Him freely and gladly
will receive grace answering to
grace.

THOMAS À KEMPIS

Spirit of Love

You will find as you look back
upon your life, that the moments
when you have really lived are the
moments when you have done
things in the spirit of love.

HENRY DRUMMOND

In the Palm of His Hand

May the road rise to meet you,
may the wind always be at your
back, the sun shine warm upon
your face. . .and until we meet
again, may God hold you in the
palm of His hand.

IRISH BLESSING

Unlimited Love

Everything which relates to God
is infinite. We must therefore,
while we keep our hearts humble,
keep our aims high. Our highest
services are indeed but finite,
imperfect. But as God is unlimited
in goodness, He should have our
unlimited love.

HANNAH MORE

Every Step

Isn't it great that God wants us
to talk to Him about all of our
worries and cares? What a gift that
He cares about everything that
happens to us every step of the way.

Love

Love makes burdens lighter,
because you divide them. It makes
joys more intense, because you
share them. It makes you stronger
so that you can reach out and
become involved with life in ways
you dared not risk alone.

Love Exalted

Joy is love exalted; peace is love
in repose; long-suffering is love
enduring; gentleness is love in
society; goodness is love in action;
faith is love on the battlefield;
meekness is love in school;
and temperance is love in training.

DWIGHT L. MOODY

Meant to Be...

Our Creator would never have
made such lovely days, and have
given us the deep hearts to enjoy
them, above and beyond all
thought, unless we were meant to
be immortal.

NATHANIEL HAWTHORNE

Complete

The happy glow that
  sharing brings,
A secret smile, a small surprise,
A special look in
  a loved one's eyes.
Comfort given, interest shown,
Quiet moments spent alone—
It's the "little things,"
  small and sweet,
That make loving so complete.

Joy in Creation

What a wildly wonderful world,
GOD! You made it all, with
Wisdom at your side, made earth
overflow with your wonderful
creations. . . . All the creatures
look expectantly to you. . . .
The glory of GOD—let it last
forever! Let GOD enjoy his
creation!

PSALM 104:24, 27, 31 MSG

A New Day

Tomorrow is a new day; begin it
well and serenely and with too
high a spirit to be cumbered with
your old nonsense. This day is all
that is good and fair. It is too dear,
with its hopes and invitations,
to waste a moment on yesterdays.

RALPH WALDO EMERSON

God's Promises

Thankfully, God is not a promise breaker. When He promised you would spend eternity with Him if you accepted the work of His Son on the cross. . .He meant it. Doesn't it bring joy to your heart to know God won't break His promises?

Never Lost

Charity is never lost: it may meet
with ingratitude, or be of no
service to those on whom it was
bestowed, yet it ever does a work of
beauty and grace upon the heart of
the giver.

CONYERS MIDDLETON

Sunny Smile

It was a sunny smile,
And little it cost in the giving.
But like morning light,
  it scattered the night,
And made the day worth living.

ANONYMOUS

Thy Will Be Done

My Jesus, as Thou wilt!
  Oh, may Thy will be mine!
Into Thy hand of love
  I would my all resign;
Through sorrow or through joy,
  conduct me as Thine own;
And help me still to say,
  "My Lord, Thy will be done."

BENJAMIN SCHMOLCK

A Rainbow

We may run, walk, stumble, drive,
or fly, but let us never lose sight of
the reason for the journey, or miss
a chance to see a rainbow on
the way.

GLORIA GAITHER

Great Blessing

Whenever you react with
praise and thanksgiving for an
opportunity to grow more like
Jesus in your way of reacting to
things, instead of grumbling or
feeling self-pity, you will find
that that whole situation will be
changed into a great blessing.

HANNAH HURNARD

At Least One

Try to make at least one person happy every day, and then in ten years you may have made three thousand six hundred and fifty persons happy, or brightened a small town by your contribution to the fund of general enjoyment.

SYDNEY SMITH

God Outdoes Himself

GOD, your God, will outdo himself in
making things go well for you. . . .
Yes, GOD will start enjoying you
again, making things go well for you
just as he enjoyed doing it for your
ancestors.

DEUTERONOMY 30:9 MSG

Lasting Satisfaction

Help me to invest my time in more
worthy pursuits, Lord, ones that
will provide lasting satisfaction.
I'm not sure what You will ask
of me, but I am willing to try
anything You recommend and give
any resulting praise to You.

Not on Marble

A good character is the best
tombstone. Those who loved
you, and were helped by you, will
remember you when the forget-
me-nots are withered. Carve
your name on hearts, and not on
marble.

CHARLES H. SPURGEON

They Just Shine

We are told to let our light shine,
and if it does, we won't need to tell
anybody it does. Lighthouses don't
fire cannons to call attention to
their shining—they just shine.

DWIGHT L. MOODY

To Cheer Travelers

Our gifts and attainments are not
only to be light and warmth in
our own dwellings, but are also to
shine through the windows into
the dark night, to guide and cheer
bewildered travelers on the road.

HENRY WARD BEECHER

All of Himself

An infinite God can give all of
Himself to each of His children.
He does not distribute Himself
that each may have a part, but to
each one He gives all of Himself
as fully as if there were no others.

A. W. TOZER

Spheres of Influence

Others are affected by what I
am and say and do. And these
others have also these spheres
of influence. So that a single act
of mine may spread in widening
circles through a nation of
humanity.

WILLIAM ELLERY CHANNING

Making Melody in Your Heart

Be filled with the Spirit; speaking
to yourselves in psalms and hymns
and spiritual songs, singing and
making melody in your heart to
the Lord; giving thanks always
for all things unto God and the
Father in the name of our Lord
Jesus Christ.

EPHESIANS 5:18–20 KJV

Heaven Breaking Through

All that is sweet, delightful,
and amiable in this world, in the
serenity of the air, the fineness of
the seasons, the joy of light,
the melody of sounds, the beauty
of colors, the fragrance of smells,
the splendor of precious stones,
is nothing else but heaven
breaking through the veil of this
world.

WILLIAM LAW

What's Your Choice?

Every morning as we slip out of
bed and slide our feet into
our warm, fluffy slippers,
we have a choice: Will we face
the circumstances and people
in our lives with grumbling and
negativity—or will we face them
with gratitude?

The Music You Hear

If a man does not keep pace
with his companions, perhaps it
is because he hears a different
drummer. Let him step to the
music which he hears, however
measured or far away.

HENRY DAVID THOREAU

Reflections

God desires that your children
walk in joy—and that starts
with you. Children are, after
all, a reflection of their parents.
Today, throw open the windows
of your home to the possibility of
everlasting joy!

Good Grasp of Life

A sense of humor. . .is needed armor. Joy in one's heart and some laughter on one's lips is a sign that the person down deep has a pretty good grasp of life.

HUGH SIDEY

Happy the Home

Happy the home
   when God is there,
And love fills every breast,
When one their wish,
   and one their prayer,
And one their heavenly rest.
Happy the home where Jesus' name
Is sweet to every ear;
Where children early
   speak His fame,
And parents hold Him dear.

HENRY WARE JR.

A Silent Witness

For many people, the heavy
responsibilities of home and
family and earning a living absorb
all their time and strength.
Yet such a home—where love is—
may be a light shining in a dark
place, a silent witness to the reality
and the love of God.

OLIVE WYON

Everything We Need

We're depending on GOD;
he's everything we need. What's
more, our hearts brim with joy
since we've taken for our own his
holy name. Love us, GOD, with
all you've got—that's what we're
depending on.

PSALM 33:20–22 MSG

I'm Free!

I'm glad God's thoughts and ways are different from mine. Without that difference, I'd be stuck in the muck of my own thinking, without escape. But today I'm free to dwell in His thoughts and actions. There's no better way to live!

Little Pleasures

Don't ever let yourself get so
busy that you miss those little
but important extras in life—the
beauty of a day. . .the smile of a
friend. . .the serenity of a quiet
moment alone. For it is often life's
smallest pleasures and gentlest joys
that make the biggest and most
lasting difference.

Hope

There is no happiness which hope
cannot surmount, no grief which
it cannot mitigate. It is the wealth
of the homeless, the health of the
sick, the freedom of the captive,
the rest of the laborer.

THEODORE LEDYARD CUYLER

Your Passions

You need to focus what energy
you have on things you are
passionate about. And you need
some level of time management
and organization to keep you from
getting distracted and wasting
yourself on the small stuff.

LEE SILBER

The Leisure of Eternity

The action of those whose lives
are given to the Spirit has in
it something of the leisure of
Eternity; and because of this,
they achieve far more than those
whose lives are enslaved by the
rush and hurry, the unceasing
tick-tick of the world.

EVELYN UNDERHILL

Everlasting Joy

Therefore the redeemed of the
LORD shall return, and come with
singing unto Zion; and everlasting
joy shall be upon their head:
they shall obtain gladness and joy;
and sorrow and mourning shall
flee away.

ISAIAH 51:11 KJV

Joyful Quality

Being playful is a joyful quality.
. . . It reminds you to not take
yourself, or the other members of
your family, too seriously. . . .
It allows you to keep your heart
open to those around you and to
bounce back from setbacks.

RICHARD CARLSON

After a Drop

Juggling, like any goal, happens
in time. . .[with] toleration and
persistence. Free from anxiety
about wild success or dismal
failure, your determination. . .can
make it all come together. . . .
After a drop, all you need to do is
pick up the balls and start throwing
again.

STEVE COHEN

Forgiveness

It's so important not to hold a grudge. It hurts you, and it hurts the one you're refusing to forgive. If you've been holding someone in unforgiveness, may today be the day when you let it go. There is incredible joy—both in forgiving and in being forgiven.

Infinitely Rich and Beautiful

I think these difficult times have helped me to understand better than before how infinitely rich and beautiful life is in every way and that so many things that one goes around worrying about are of no importance whatsoever.

Isak Dinesen

Never in a Hurry

Christ was never in a hurry.
There was no rushing forward,
no anticipating, no fretting over
what might be. Each day's duties
were done as every day brought
them, and the rest was left to God.

MARY SLESSOR

Life-Infusing Laughter

If we wrestle free to embrace the
concept that something about
God's gift of laughter is primal and
life infusing, we have a fighting
chance to rise above the troubles
that threaten to steal our joy.

What You Want

Often people attempt to live their
lives backwards: they try to have
more things, or more money,
in order to do more of what they
want so that they will be happier.
The way it actually works is the
reverse. You must first be who you
really are, then, do what you need
to do, in order to have what you
want.

MARGARET YOUNG

Wonders

Many, O LORD my God, are the
wonders you have done. The things
you planned for us no one can
recount to you; were I to speak
and tell of them, they would be too
many to declare.

PSALM 40:5 NIV

Live Each Day to the Fullest

It's only when we truly know and
understand that we have a limited
time on earth—and that we have
no way of knowing when our time
is up—that we will begin to live
each day to the fullest, as if it was
the only one we had.

ELISABETH KÜBLER-ROSS

You Love Me, Lord

You love the short, the impaired,
those who struggle with life and
sometimes go under. You love me,
Lord, so much that You call me
forth by name and beautify me with
Your salvation, the most precious
ornament I could ever wish for.

Watering Others

To make ourselves happy, we must
make others happy. . .in order
to become spiritually vigorous,
we must seek the spiritual good
of others. In watering others,
we ourselves are watered.

CHARLES SPURGEON

No Two Alike!

Think of it—not one whorled
finger exactly like another!
If God should take such delight
in designing fingertips, think how
much pleasure the unfurling of
your life must give Him.

LUCIE CHRISTOPHER

Today Is Your Best Day

As God's child, today is your best
day because you are totally and
completely dependent upon Him.
. . . God is your only rock, your
only security, your only certainty,
and your only hope.

ROY LESSIN

Be True

God knew how much the world
needed your smile, your hands,
your voice, your way of thinking,
your insights, your love.
God speaks through you in a way
He can through no other. Be true
to the person He created.

GWYNETH GAVIN

He Is Close

We do not need to search for heaven over here or over there in order to find our eternal Father. In fact, we do not even need to speak out loud, for though we speak in the smallest whisper or the most fleeting thought, He is close enough to hear us.

ST. TERESA OF AVILA

Green Again

Sometimes our fate resembles a
fruit tree in winter. Who would
think at beholding such a sad
sight that those jagged twigs will
turn green again in the spring and
blossom and bear fruit, but we
hope it, we know it.

JOHANN WOLFGANG VON GOETHE

Creator of Laughter

Spend some quiet time each day
with the Creator of laughter.
Let your heart overflow as He fills
up your endorphin tank, equipping
you to face the serious side of life
with grace and courage.

RACHEL ST. JOHN-GILBERT

Bound to Act

As soon as He finds you ready,
God is bound to act, bound to
pour Himself into your being,
just as, when the air is pure and
clear, the sun must pour into it
without holding back.

MEISTER ECKHART

Season of Favor

God takes great pleasure in you
and wants to bless you above all
you could ask or think. So, when
you're in a season of favor, praise
Him. Shout for joy and be glad!
Tell others about the great things
the Lord has done.

The Way to Happiness

The way to happiness: Keep your heart free from hate, your mind from worry. Live simply, expect little, give much. Fill your life with love. Scatter sunshine. Forget self, think of others. Do as you would be done by.

H. C. MATTERN

From Within

Happiness is the greatest paradox
in nature. It can grow in any soil,
live under any conditions.
It defies environment. The reason
for this is that it does not come
from without but from within.
Whenever you see a person seeking
happiness outside himself, you can
be sure he has never yet found it.

FORMAN LINCICOME

Peace, Quiet, Joy. . .

The more a man gives up his heart
to God, to his vocation, and to
men, forgetful of himself and of
that which belongs to him—the
greater poise he will acquire, until
he reaches peace, quiet, joy.

ALEXANDER YELCHANINOV

Hallelujah!

"Hallelujah! For the Lord our
God, the Almighty, reigns. Let us
rejoice and be glad and give the
glory to Him, for the marriage of
the Lamb has come and His bride
has made herself ready."

REVELATION 19:6–7 NASB

Stars

Stars may be seen from the
bottom of a deep well, when they
cannot be discovered from the top
of a mountain, so are many things
learned in adversity which the
prosperous man dreams not of.

CHARLES SPURGEON

Many Joys

The idea that many people
have that life is a vale of tears
is just as false as the idea which
the great majority have, and to
which youth, health, and wealth
incline you, that life is a place
of entertainment. Life is a place
of service, where one sometimes
has occasion to put up with a lot
that is hard, but more often to
experience many joys.

LEO TOLSTOY

Pathway to Happiness

When we start to count flowers,
  we cease to count weeds;
When we start to count blessings,
  we cease to count needs;
When we start to count laughter,
  we cease to count tears;
When we start to count memories,
  we cease to count years.

Finding Joy

There are those who suffer greatly,
and yet, through the recognition
that pain can be a thread in the
pattern of God's weaving, find the
way to a fundamental joy.

Pleasant Things

I know nothing so pleasant as to
sit there on a summer afternoon,
with the western sun flickering
through the great elder-tree
. . .where flowers and flowering
shrubs are set as thick as grass in
a field, a wilderness of blossom,
interwoven, intertwined, wreathy,
garlandy, profuse beyond all
profusion.

MARY MITFORD

Unique Circle of Influence

The next time you're tempted to
covet the good life, think again.
Compared to many people, you're
probably already living it. Why not
try hard to be thankful for all God
has given you? Decide to make
an impact for Him in the unique
circle of influence where He has
placed you.

Marvelous Things

O LORD, you are my God; I will
exalt you and praise your name,
for in perfect faithfulness you have
done marvelous things, things
planned long ago.

ISAIAH 25:1 NIV

Peaceful

The first step in becoming a more
peaceful person is to have the
humility to admit that, in most
cases, you're creating your own
emergencies. Life will usually go
on if things don't go according to
plan.

RICHARD CARLSON

Make Me an Instrument

O Lord, make me an instrument
of Thy peace; where there is
hatred, let me sow love;
where there is injury, pardon;
where there is doubt, faith; where
there is despair, hope; where there
is darkness, light; and where there
is sadness, joy.

St. Francis of Assisi

Wait

Learn but in quietness and
stillness to retire to the Lord,
and wait upon Him; in whom thou
shalt find peace and joy, in the
midst of thy trouble from the cruel
and vexatious spirit of this world.
So wait to know thy work and
service to the Lord every day
. . .and thou wilt want neither help,
support, or comfort.

ISAAC PENINGTON

Richness of Life

Oh do not pray for easy lives,
pray to be strong men and women.
Do not pray for tasks equal to your
powers. Pray for powers equal to
your tasks. Then the doing of your
work will be no miracle, but you
shall be the miracle. Every day you
shall wonder at yourself, at the
richness of life which has come to
you by the grace of God.

PHILLIPS BROOKS

Its Own Reward

He that does good to another does
good also to himself, not only in
the consequence but in the very
act. For the consciousness of
well-doing is in itself ample
reward.

LUCIUS ANNAEUS SENECA

A Joyful Tomorrow

We have our ups and downs—
our sorrows and our joys—but
God remains consistent, never
changing. We weep in the bad
times and celebrate during the
good. Oh, if only we could
remember that on the tail end
of every sorrow, there is a joyful
tomorrow!

A Great Secret

Doing nothing for others is the undoing of one's self. We must be purposely kind and generous, or we miss the best part of existence. The heart that goes out of itself gets large and full of joy. This is the great secret of the inner life. We do ourselves the most good doing something for others.

HORACE MANN

Love Is the Foundation

All true morality, inward and
outward, is comprehended in love,
for love is the foundation of all
the commandments. . . . There is
no inner freedom which does not
manifest itself in works of love.

MEISTER ECKHART

Joy in Religion

The trouble with many men is that
they have got just enough religion
to make them miserable. If there is
not joy in religion, you have got a
leak in your religion.

BILLY SUNDAY

Forgiven

We need not climb up into
heaven to see whether our sins
are forgiven: Let us look into our
hearts, and see if we can forgive
others. If we can, we need not
doubt but God has forgiven us.

THOMAS WATSON

A Blessing

Father, fill our hearts full of You
and Your Word; then we can sing
with grace and joy. My family and
I can proclaim Your goodness to
all those we meet. What a blessing!

Good Samaritans

As we travel life's earthly road
from Jerusalem to Jericho may
we be Good Samaritans to all
who need us, cheering, healing,
and fortifying them with true
neighborliness, vitalizing all the
relations of life with an unselfish
love, remembering that love is the
strongest force in the world.

GEORGE W. TRUETT

Thou Shalt Be Served Thyself

A child's kiss,
Set on thy sighing lips,
  shall make thee glad;
A poor man served by thee,
  shall make thee rich;
A sick man helped by thee,
  shall make thee strong,
Thou shalt be served thyself
  by every sense
Of service which thou renderest.

ELIZABETH BARRETT BROWNING

Live Exuberantly

Love GOD, your God. Walk in his
ways. Keep his commandments,
regulations, and rules so that
you will live, really live, live
exuberantly, blessed by GOD, your
God.

DEUTERONOMY 30:16 MSG

Be Truly Happy

I don't know what your destiny
will be, but one thing I know:
The only ones among you who
will be truly happy are those who
will have sought and found how to
serve.

ALBERT SCHWEITZER

Follow His Lead

Too many choices at pivotal points in life can leave us feeling like confused coffee nerds—mouths hanging open at the Starbucks counter. Frozen in time, we may wonder, *What do I do now? What if I make a mistake and place the wrong order? What if I make a fool of myself?* At those times we need to take a deep breath, put our hands in God's, and follow His lead.

RACHEL ST. JOHN-GILBERT

Gifts of Ourselves

The greatest gifts we can give to others are not material things but gifts of ourselves. The great gifts are those of love, of inspiration, of kindness, of encouragement, of forgiveness, of ideas and ideals. How many great gifts can we give this day? Each day let's do someone a good turn—one that will either not be discovered or will be discovered only by accident.

MARGUERITE HARMON BRO

Restful Enjoyment

May the God of love and peace set
your heart at rest and speed you on
your journey. May He meanwhile
shelter you. . .in the security of
trust and in the restful enjoyment
of His riches.

RAYMOND OF PENYAFORT

Peace That Passes All Understanding

What is meant by the peace that
passes all understanding? It does
not mean a peace no one can
comprehend. It means a peace no
amount of reasoning will bring. . . .
Your heart can rest in perfect security
because God knows, He loves, He
leads.

A. B. SIMPSON

A Cottage

Are you not surprised to find
how independent of money peace
of conscience is and how much
happiness can be condensed in
the humblest home? A cottage
will not hold the bulky furniture
and sumptuous accommodations
of a mansion; but if God be
there, a cottage will hold as much
happiness as might stock a palace.

JAMES HAMILTON

Incredible Wealth

Home and family can bring
us incredible wealth. Who can
be richer than those who have
shared joy-filled times,
who have known the gifts of love
and companionship, and who
carry within them a treasure chest
filled with cherished memories.

ROY LESSIN

You Are Loved!

You are loved. . .incredibly,
sacrificially loved by the King of
kings. Doesn't that fill you with
overwhelming joy? Can you sense
His heart for you? You are loved
today and always!

His Glory

There is a signature of wisdom and power impressed on the works of God, which evidently distinguishes them from the feeble imitations of men. Not only the splendor of the sun, but the glimmering light of the glowworm proclaims His glory.

JOHN NEWTON

He Never Tires of Hearing from You

Start out your day by talking to
God. Go through your day talking
to God. End your day talking to
God. He is the One who never
tires of hearing your voice, and He
can wipe away all tears from your
eyes.

JOYCE LIVINGSTON

Mourning into Dancing

You have turned my mourning into dancing; you have taken off my sackcloth and clothed me with joy, so that my soul may praise you and not be silent. O LORD my God, I will give thanks to you forever.

PSALM 30:11–12 NRSV

Wonderful Things

God has wonderful things in mind for you. If you ask, He'll show you what gifts He's given you and how He wants you to impact others with them. Don't wait until eternity to experience the joys and delights of faith—share some of that good news today!

Light

However things may appear to be,
of all possible circumstances, those
circumstances in whose midst I
am set, these are the best that He
could choose for me. We do not
know how this is true—where
would faith be if we did?—but
we do know that all things that
happen are full of shining seed.
Light is sown for us, not darkness.

A Full Heart

If your heart is full from the
blessings God has rained on you
lately, revel in this season of joy
and let your laughter reverberate
to the heavens.

Take Each Day Slowly

Life is full of daily treasures.
The wave of a neighbor, the smell
of a fresh spring rain, a hug from a
child. Take each day slowly so that
each treasure you find can be a
source of joy to fill your heart.

MELISSA JOHNSON

Rejoice Always!

Rejoice in the Lord always.
I will say it again: Rejoice! Let
your gentleness be evident to
all. The Lord is near. Do not be
anxious about anything, but in
everything, by prayer and petition,
with thanksgiving, present your
requests to God.

PHILIPPIANS 4:4–6 NIV

Deep Springs of Life

Youth is not a time of life; it is a
state of mind; it is not a matter of
rosy cheeks, red lips, and supple
knees; it is a matter of the will,
quality of the imagination, a vigor
of the emotions; it is the freshness
of the deep springs of life.

SAMUEL ULLMAN

Rest

The Lord designed our bodies to
require rest, and if we skip that
part of the equation, we suffer
the consequences! If you want
your body to confidently dwell in
safety, then you must get the rest
you need. Rest makes for a happy
heart. . .and a healthy body.

Explore, Dream, Discover!

Twenty years from now you will be more disappointed by the things that you didn't do than by the ones you did do. So throw off the bowlines. Sail away from the safe harbor. Catch the trade winds in your sails. Explore. Dream. Discover.

MARK TWAIN

Bend to Every Necessity

Faith, like light, should always be
simple and unbending; while love,
like warmth, should beam forth
on every side and bend to every
necessity of our brethren.

MARTIN LUTHER

Companion and Friend

Are you alone? . . . Do you feel
as if no one cares? Take heart,
friend. God cares. He loves you.
His loving arms are always open to
you. Let Him be your companion
and your friend.

JOYCE LIVINGSTON

His Joy in You

God created you. He knows you
and every aspect of you. His love
for you is boundless, and His joy
in you comes full circle each time
you call Him into your life in
prayer.

KAREN MOORE

Treasures

When God finds a soul that rests
in Him and is not easily moved,
He operates within it in His own
manner. . . . He gives to such a
soul the key to the treasures He
has prepared for it so that it might
enjoy them. And to this same soul
He gives the joy of His presence
which entirely absorbs such a soul.

CATHERINE OF GENOA

A Righteous Heart...

If there is righteousness in the
heart, there will be beauty in the
character. If there is beauty in
the character, if there is harmony
in the home, there will be order in
the nation. When there is order
in the nation, there will be peace
in the world.

CHINESE PROVERB

The Sun Will Shine

"Because of the tender mercy of our God. . .the rising sun will come to us from heaven to shine on those living in darkness and in the shadow of death, to guide our feet into the path of peace."

LUKE 1:78–79 NIV

A Practical Beginning

So never lose an opportunity
of urging a practical beginning,
however small, for it is wonderful
how often in such matters the
mustard-seed germinates and
roots itself.

FLORENCE NIGHTINGALE

Opportunity

Jesus, please bring new
opportunities for God-filled
relationships into my life today.
I want You to use me to bless others
and bring them closer to You.

Rewarding Joy

The marvelous richness of human experience would lose something of rewarding joy if there were no limitations to overcome.
The hilltop hour would not be half so wonderful if there were no dark valleys to traverse.

HELEN KELLER

Dream Come True

Often we find joy in simply
speaking aloud those things that
make our hearts flutter. If we can
learn to hold our desires loosely
and let God sift them through His
all-knowing, all-loving hands, we
will probably find some dreams
coming true.

For the Love of God

The heart is rich when it is
content, and it is always content
when its desires are fixed on
God. Nothing can bring greater
happiness than doing God's will
for the love of God.

MIGUEL FEBRES CORDERO-MUÑOZ

Shine!

Dear Lord, thank You for my
home. I ask that You fill it with
Your Holy Spirit. Even when I
don't have time to polish and
dust, may it still shine with Your
welcome and love, so that whoever
comes in my doors senses that You
are present.

ELLYN SANNA

Creative Purpose

God's great purpose for the human
race [is] that He created us for
Himself. This realization of our
election by God is the most joyful
on earth, and we must learn to
rely on this tremendous creative
purpose of God.

OSWALD CHAMBERS

Comforting Thoughts

For each of us the time is surely
coming when we shall have
nothing but God. Health and
wealth and friends and hiding
places will all be swept away. . . .
To the man of pseudo faith that
is a terrifying thought, but to
real faith it is one of the most
comforting thoughts the heart can
entertain.

A. W. TOZER

Draw Near

Every time you draw near to God,
He offers you the opportunity to
see Him. To find Him. To trust
Him. Let Him give you His joyous
perspective today.

Believe. . .

Faith is the root of all blessings.
Believe, and you shall be saved;
believe, and your needs must be
satisfied; believe, and you cannot
but be comforted and happy.

JEREMY TAYLOR

No Greater Trust

I will not doubt,
   though all my ships at sea
Come drifting home
   with broken masts and sails;
I shall believe the hand
   which never fails,
From seeming evil worketh
   good to me.
And, though I weep because those
   sails are battered,
Still will I cry, while
   my best hopes lie shattered,
"I trust in Thee."

ELLA WHEELER WILCOX

From Within

All God's glory and beauty come
from within, and there He delights
to dwell. His visits there are
frequent, His conversations sweet,
His comforts refreshing, His peace
passing all understanding.

THOMAS À KEMPIS

As Your Faith Is Strengthened

As your faith is strengthened you
will find that there is no longer the
need to have a sense of control,
that things will flow as they will,
and that you will flow with them,
to your great delight and benefit.

EMMANUEL TENEY

Life Flows

The more I learn, the more I
realize life is not about what
you conquer with your will but
rather submitting your will to the
natural energies God has created
all around us. Life flows if we are
brave enough to open to it.

WILLOW CLARE SMITH

A Morning Star

From far beyond our world of
trouble and care and change, our
Lord shines with undimmed light,
a radiant, guiding Star to all who
will follow Him—a morning Star,
promise of a better day.

CHARLES E. HURLBURT AND T. C. HORTON

A Put-Together Life

But now that you've found you
don't have to listen to sin tell you
what to do, and have discovered
the delight of listening to God
telling you, what a surprise! A
whole, healed, put-together life
right now.

ROMANS 6:22 MSG

Little Things

Thank You, God, for little things
   that often come our way,
The things we take for granted but
   don't mention when we pray.
The unexpected courtesy,
   the thoughtful, kindly deed,
A hand reached out to help us
   in the time of sudden need.

Shared Joys

If you've been waiting for heaven
to enjoy all the joys and delights
of faith, turn around. Look at the
blessings you've received today,
all the things God has done and is
doing in your life, and appreciate
them. But don't stop there. . . .
Because God never gives us
blessings simply to enjoy—every
good thing is meant to be shared.

Sing!

May none of God's wonderful
works keep silence, night or
morning. Bright stars, high
mountains, the depths of the seas,
sources of rushing rivers: May all
these break into song as we sing to
the Father.

Blessing upon Blessing

God, who is love—who is, if I
may say it this way, made out of
love—simply cannot help but shed
blessing on blessing upon us.
We do not need to beg, for He
simply cannot help it!

HANNAH WHITALL SMITH

Surprised by Laughter

When we're feeling down, lonely,
or in need of inspiration,
we may find ourselves surprised by
laughter and better able to cope
again. And best of all, we may find
ourselves, as C. S. Lewis wrote,
"surprised by joy"—the joy that
inevitably comes from yielding our
lives to God.

Lilies of the Field

"And why are you worried about clothing? Observe how the lilies of the field grow; they do not toil nor do they spin, yet I say to you that not even Solomon in all his glory clothed himself like one of these."

MATTHEW 6:28–29 NASB

Unexpected Joys

Oh, what hope lies in the unseen tomorrow! What unexpected joys are just around the corner. Sure, you can't see them. . .but they're there! Before you give in to fear, allow the Lord to transform your mind. See tomorrow as He sees it filled with unexpected joys.

How Beautiful!

How beautiful it is to be alive!
To wake each morn as if the
Maker's grace did us afresh
from nothingness derive,
that we might sing
"How happy is our case!
How beautiful it is to be alive."

HENRY SEPTIMUS SUTTON

He Is Seeking You More

If you are seeking after God, you
may be sure of this: God is seeking
you much more. He is the Lover,
and you are His beloved. He has
promised Himself to you.

John of the Cross

A Great Deal

The one who truly loves in spirit. . .
cares nothing whether he receives
the affection of another or not. . . .
Those who learn to love for the sake
of God's love will love others a great
deal. They will love with greater
compassion and greater intensity.

ST. TERESA OF AVILA

Value of Love

When we love someone, we want
to be with them, and we view their
love for us with great honor even
if they are not a person of great
rank. For this reason—and not
because of our great rank—God
values our love. So much, in fact,
that He suffered greatly on our
behalf.

JOHN CHRYSOSTOM

God's Gifts

Gratitude consists in a watchful,
minute attention to the particulars
of our state, and to the multitude
of God's gifts, taken one by one.
It fills us with a consciousness that
God loves and cares for us, even to
the least event and smallest need
of life.

HENRY EDWARD MANNING

World without End

Bring us, O Lord God. . .to enter
into that gate and dwell in that
house, where there shall be no
darkness nor dazzling, but one
equal light; no noise nor silence,
but one equal music. . .no ends nor
beginnings, but one equal eternity;
in the habitations of Your majesty
and Your glory, world without end.

JOHN DONNE

Remain Forever

It is good to be with Jesus and to
remain here for ever. What greater
happiness or higher honor could
we have than to be with God, to be
made like Him and to live in His
light?

ANASTASIUS OF SINAI

A Thirty-One-Flavors World!

Do you really think God wants us
to live a vanilla-bland life when
He's made a thirty-one-flavors
world? God wants us to color our
world with rainbow colors and
Willy Wonka flavors. Sure, playing
it safe can make life easier (and
duller), but branching out—even
a little—can make life fuller (and
funner).

RACHEL ST. JOHN-GILBERT

His Generosity

You can be sure that God will take
care of everything you need,
his generosity exceeding even
yours in the glory that pours
from Jesus. Our God and Father
abounds in glory that just pours
out into eternity.

PHILIPPIANS 4:19–20 MSG

Wellspring of Joy

Father, when happiness is hard
to come by, help me to learn to
draw more consistently on Your
wellspring of joy. Help me delight
in the little gifts You bring my way
every day.

Warm, Gentle Sunshine

May God send His love like
sunshine in His warm and
gentle way,
To fill each corner of your heart
each moment of today.
His overflowing love delights to
make us partakers of the
bounties He graciously imparts.

HANNAH MORE

Praise

O God, great and wonderful,
who has created the heavens,
dwelling in the light and beauty
of it; who has made the earth,
revealing Yourself in every flower
that opens; let not my eyes be
blind to You, neither my heart be
dead, but teach me to praise You,
even as the lark which offers her
song at daybreak.

ISIDORE OF SEVILLE

Radiant Sun

Why should we live halfway up the
hill and swathed in the mists, when
we might have an unclouded sky
and a radiant sun over our heads if
we would climb higher and walk in
the light of His face?

ALEXANDER MACLAREN

Strength

The same God who guides the
stars in their courses, who directs
the earth in its orbit, who feeds
the burning furnace of the sun
and keeps the stars perpetually
burning with their fires—the same
God has promised to supply thy
strength.

C. S. LEWIS

Great and Good Things

It is only by thinking about great
and good things that we come to
love them; and it is only by loving
them that we come to long for
them; and it is only by longing
for them that we are impelled to
seek after them; and it is only
by seeking after them that they
become ours.

HENRY VAN DYKE

The Thankful Heart

When all else is gone, God is left, and nothing changes Him. Let the thankful heart sweep through the day, and, as the magnet finds the iron, so it will find in every hour some heavenly blessing; only the iron in God's hand is gold.

HENRY WARD BEECHER

Something to Laugh About

When our human frailties
break through in waves of the
ridiculous, God's mercy prevails.
After all, to be human isn't a sin,
but to pretend we're not is really
something to laugh about.

TINA KRAUSE

Affectionate Conversation

If you and I are going to enjoy
the peace of paradise during this
life, we must become accustomed
to a familiar, humble, and very
affectionate conversation with the
Lord Jesus.

BROTHER LAWRENCE

The Right Choice

Pause for a moment and
remember: This is the day the
Lord has brought about. I will
rejoice! It's His day, and He longs
for me to spend time with Him.
Rejoice! It's the right choice.

Bounteous God

O may this bounteous God
   through all our life be near us,
With ever joyful hearts and
   blessed peace to cheer us;
And keep us in His grace,
   and guide us when perplexed,
And free us from all ills
   in this world and the next.

MARTIN RINKART

It's Up to You

Between the house and the
store there are little pockets of
happiness. A bird, a garden, a
friend's greeting, a child's smile,
a cat in the sunshine needing a
stroke. Recognize them or ignore
them. It's always up to you.

PAM BROWN

More Than Meets the Eye

Ordinary things have a great
power to reveal the mysterious
nearness of a caring, liberating
God. . . . In what seems ordinary
and everyday there is always more
than at first meets the eye.

CHARLES CUMMINGS

Hope in God

Why art thou cast down, O my soul? and why art thou disquieted within me? hope in God: for I shall yet praise him, who is the health of my countenance, and my God.

PSALM 43:5 KJV

Forward Joyously

A new life begins for us with every second. Let us go forward joyously to meet it. We must press on, whether we will or no, and we shall walk better with our eyes before us than with them ever cast behind.

Fresh Courage

Be patient with everyone, but
above all with thyself. I mean,
do not be disheartened by your
imperfections, but always rise up
with fresh courage.

FRANCIS DE SALES

Share with Him

Has prayer become mechanical, a
chore instead of a joy? Remember
how beloved you are by the One
you're speaking to. He doesn't
want to hear the details of just
anyone's life—He's asked you to
share with Him, and you're blessed
to know His love.

Prayer for Joy

Give me work to do;
  give me health;
Give me joy in simple things.
Give me an eye for beauty,
A tongue for truth,
  a heart that loves,
A mind that reasons,
  a sympathy that understands.

Beautifully Drest

Great wide, beautiful,
  wonderful world,
With the wonderful waters
  round you curled,
And the wonderful grass
  upon your breast,
World, you are beautifully drest.

WILLIAM BRIGHTLY RANDS

Step Out

When you come to the edge of all
the light you have, and you must
take a step into the darkness of the
unknown, believe that one of two
things will happen. Either there
will be something solid for you to
stand on—or you will be taught
how to fly.

PATRICK OVERTON

Sing

Be like the bird that,
  halting in its flight
Awhile on boughs too slight,
Feels them give way beneath her,
  and yet sings
Knowing that she hath wings.

VICTOR HUGO

Praise Ye the Lord

Praise ye the LORD. Praise God in his sanctuary: praise him in the firmament of his power. Praise him for his mighty acts: praise him according to his excellent greatness. . . . Let every thing that hath breath praise the LORD. Praise ye the LORD.

PSALM 150:1–2, 6 KJV

Soar!

We look at our burdens and heavy
loads and shrink from them; but as
we lift them and bind them about
our hearts, they become wings;
and on them we rise and soar
toward God.

MRS. CHARLES E. COWMAN

Limitless Hope

When we take time to notice the
simple things in life, we never lack
for encouragement. We discover
we are surrounded by limitless
hope that's just wearing everyday
clothes.

From the Inside Out

Can you really look beyond your grief to find the joy? Our very strength comes from the joy God places inside us, and we need that strength even more when we're facing seemingly impossible odds! Today, may God's joy strengthen you from the inside out.

Moving toward Peace and Joy

God came to us because God
wanted to join us on the road,
to listen to our story, and to help
us realize that we are not walking
in circles but moving toward the
house of peace and joy.

THOMAS MERTON

Spread Love

Spread love everywhere you go:
first of all in your own house.
Give love to your children, to your
wife or husband, to a next-door
neighbor. . . . Let no one ever
come to you without leaving
better and happier.

MOTHER TERESA

Nourishing Love

This is the miracle that happens
every time to those who really
love; the more they give, the more
they possess of that precious
nourishing love from which
flowers and children have their
strength.

RAINER MARIA RILKE

Step Out with the One Who Knows All

Your heart is beating with God's love; open it to others. He has entrusted you with gifts and talents; use them for His service. He goes before you each step of the way; walk in faith. Take courage. Step out into the unknown with the One who knows all.

ELLYN SANNA

Play

The real joy of life is in its play.
Play is anything we do for the joy
and love of doing it, apart from
any profit, compulsion, or sense of
duty. It is the real living of life.

WALTER RAUSCHENBUSCH

Expect Hope

Expect to have hope rekindled.
Expect your prayers to be answered
in wondrous ways. The dry seasons
in life do not last. The spring rains
will come again.

SARAH BAN BREATHNACH

My Season

Father, help me to have patience,
knowing my season is coming
according to Your timetable
and trusting that with Your help,
every fruit I produce will be good.

Whispers of Angel Wings

Today I stumbled and once again
Was lifted by an unseen hand.
What comfort and joy that
    knowledge brings
For I hear the whisper
    of angel wings.

ANONYMOUS

Interdependence

With independence, you get you,
yourself, and, well, you again.
But interdependence gives us
the opportunity to share the
abundance that God has given us
or to receive from someone else's
abundance. And often we make a
new friend along the way.

Overflowing

So then, just as you received
Christ Jesus as Lord, continue to
live in him, rooted and built up in
him, strengthened in the faith as
you were taught, and overflowing
with thankfulness.

COLOSSIANS 2:6–7 NIV

Best Things

The best things are nearest: breath
in your nostrils, light in your eyes,
flowers at your feet, duties at your
hand, the path of right just before
you. Do not grasp at the stars,
but do life's plain common work as
it comes, certain that daily duties
and daily bread are the sweetest
things in life.

ROBERT LOUIS STEVENSON

Possibility

An optimist is a person who sees
only the lights in the picture,
whereas a pessimist sees only the
shadows. An idealist, however,
is one who sees the light and the
shadows, but in addition sees
something else: the possibility of
changing the picture, of making
the lights prevail over the shadows.

Felix Adler

Valuable

We are of such value to God that
He came to live among us. . .and
to guide us home. He will go to
any length to seek us, even to
being lifted high upon the cross to
draw us back to Himself. We can
only respond by loving God for
His love.

CATHERINE OF SIENA

Life's Pattern

Take your needle, my child,
and work at your pattern; it will
come out a rose by and by.
Life is like that; one stitch at
a time taken patiently, and the
pattern will come out all right,
like embroidery.

OLIVER WENDELL HOLMES

Reach Out

We need to make a conscious
effort each morning to reach out
to God. . .to ask Him to satisfy
us with His mercy, His loving-
kindness. If we're truly satisfied,
joy will come. And joy is the best
antiwrinkle cream on the market.

Rewards of the Simple Life

To find the universal elements
enough; to find the air and the
water exhilarating; to be refreshed
by a morning walk or an evening
saunter. . .to be thrilled by the
stars at night; to be elated over
a bird's nest or a wildflower in
spring—these are some of the
rewards of the simple life.

JOHN BURROUGHS

A Fresh Start

Roughly translated, Psalm 103:12 assures believers that God is—figuratively speaking—following us around with a heavy-duty trash bag, ever ready to take our unkind words. . .and every other sin to the Great Landfill of things forgiven and forgotten. Sometimes we need to remember it's time to. . .make a fresh start as new creations in Christ.

Joy of Achievement

Happiness lies not in the mere
possession of money; it lies in the
joy of achievement, in the thrill of
creative effort. The joy and moral
stimulation of work no longer
must be forgotten in the mad
chase of evanescent profits.

FRANKLIN D. ROOSEVELT

We Must Sail

I find the great thing in this world is not so much where we stand, as in what direction we are moving. To reach the port of heaven, we must sail sometimes with the wind and sometimes against it—but we must sail, and not drift, nor lie at anchor.

OLIVER WENDELL HOLMES

A Magic Light

Dark as my path may seem to
others, I carry a magic light in my
heart. Faith, the spiritual strong
searchlight, illumines the way, and
although sinister doubts lurk in
the shadow, I walk unafraid toward
the enchanted wood where the
foliage is always green, where joy
abides. . .in the presence of the
Lord.

HELEN KELLER

Rest

Rest is not idleness, and to lie
sometimes on the grass on a
summer day listening to the
murmur of water, or watching
the clouds float across the sky,
is hardly a waste of time.

JOHN LUBBOCK

Rest for Your Soul

"Come to me, all you who are weary and burdened, and I will give you rest. Take my yoke upon you and learn from me, for I am gentle and humble in heart, and you will find rest for your souls. For my yoke is easy and my burden is light."

MATTHEW 11:28–30 NIV

Complete Joy

The God of the universe—the
One who created everything and
holds it all in His hands—created
each of us in His image, to bear
His likeness, His imprint. It is
only when Christ dwells within
our hearts, radiating the pure light
of His love through our humanity,
that we discover who we are and
what we were intended to be.
There is no other joy that reaches
as deep or as wide or as high—
there is no other joy that is more
complete.

Never Alone

When you face difficult days,
as all people do, you won't stand
alone. Trouble won't blast your life
but will strengthen you instead.
Your Creator can turn all trials to
blessing, if you just stand firm in
Him. Enjoy your days in Jesus.

Without Love . . .

Love is something like the clouds
that were in the sky before the sun
came out. . . . You cannot touch
the clouds, you know; but you feel
the rain and know how glad the
flowers are to have it after a hot
day. You cannot touch love either;
but you feel the sweetness that it
pours into everything. Without
love you would not be happy.

ANNIE SULLIVAN

Brighten into Eternity

If we work upon marble, it will
perish; if we work upon brass, time
will efface it; if we rear temples,
they will crumble into dust; but if
we work upon immortal minds and
instill into them just principles,
we are then engraving that upon
tablets which no time will efface,
but will brighten and brighten to
all eternity.

DANIEL WEBSTER

River of Delights

How priceless is your unfailing
love! Both high and low among
men find refuge in the shadow
of your wings. They feast on the
abundance of your house;
you give them drink from your
river of delights. For with you is
the fountain of life; in your light
we see light.

PSALM 36:7–9 NIV

Strength of Cheerfulness

Wondrous is the strength of
cheerfulness, and its power of
endurance—the cheerful man will
do more in the same time, will do
it better, will preserve it longer,
than the sad or sullen.

THOMAS CARLYLE

Knowing God

I cannot help thinking that the
best way of knowing God is to love
many things. Love this friend,
this person, this thing, whatever
you like, and you will be on the
right road to understanding Him
better.

VINCENT VAN GOGH

Praise You, Lord!

The thought of You stirs us so
deeply that we cannot be content
unless we praise You, because You
have made us for Yourself and our
hearts find no peace until they rest
in You.

ST. AUGUSTINE

Promises Kept

We may. . .depend upon God's
promises, for. . .He will be as good
as His word. He is so kind that He
cannot deceive us, so true that He
cannot break His promise.

MATTHEW HENRY

God Uses Humor

God often uses humor to show
us He's a real person with a full
range of emotions—and we can
feel closer to Him for having
made us laugh. . . . The Creator
can rain down all kinds of things
from heaven to get His children's
attention and prompt their prayers
and praise.

The Finish Line

Instead of focusing on the ups and downs of the journey, we should be looking ahead to the finish line. We want to be people who finish well. Today, set your sights on that unseen line that lies ahead. What joy will come when you cross it!

A Spark

Our lives are not determined by
what happens to us but by how we
react to what happens, not by what
life brings to us, but by the attitude
we bring to life. A positive attitude
causes a chain reaction of positive
thoughts, events, and outcomes.
It is a catalyst, a spark that creates
extraordinary results.

Singin' in the Rain

Anyone can sing in the sunshine.
You and I should sing on when the
sun has gone down or when clouds
pour out their rain, for Christ is
with us.

The Lord Bless You

"The LORD bless you and keep
you; the LORD make his face shine
upon you and be gracious to you;
the LORD turn his face toward you
and give you peace."

NUMBERS 6:24–26 NIV

A Gentle Spirit

Lord, direct me daily to accept
and apply the strength that You've
offered, so that I will truly have
the gentle spirit that You intended
me to have. Thank You, Jesus, that
I don't have to do this on my own.

Satisfaction

Look at a day when you are
supremely satisfied at the end.
It's not a day when you lounge
around doing nothing; it's when
you had everything to do, and
you've done it.

MARGARET THATCHER

Now Is the Time

If there's something special you
want to do, now is the time. If you
want to make a difference in the
world, now is the time. Don't be
fooled into thinking you should
wait until you are older or wiser or
more "secure," because it doesn't
work that way. The wisdom will
come. The security will come.
But first you must begin your
adventure.

RON ATCHISON

God's Peace

We can say, "Lord, I'm going to live this day one moment at a time, endeavoring to do what You want me to do. But I'm putting You in charge, not me." It's amazing the peace that floods our hearts—God's peace—as we turn over the responsibility to Him.

MARLA TIPTON

Calvary's Love

If monotony tries me, and I
cannot stand drudgery; if stupid
people fret me and little ruffles set
me on edge; if I make much of the
trifles of life, then I know nothing
of Calvary's love.

AMY CARMICHAEL

Especially You!

Everyone has a unique role to fill
in the world and is important in
some respect. Everyone, including
and perhaps especially you, is
indispensable.

NATHANIEL HAWTHORNE

Precious Minutes

When you look back on the years
God has ordained for you, what
will you see? I pray that you will be
able to find joy and beauty in the
most trivial of things because you
have spent those precious minutes
with God.

LORI SHANKLE

The Seasons

There is something satisfying,
rejuvenating, comforting about
the seasons. They remind me that
I play one small part in a much
bigger picture—that there is a
pulse, a sequence, a journey set
into motion by the very hand of
God Himself.

KAREN SCALF LINAMEN

Sense of the Beautiful

A person should hear a little
music, read a little poetry,
and see a fine picture every day
of their life, in order that worldly
cares may not obliterate the sense
of the beautiful which God has
implanted in the human soul.

JOHANN WOLFGANG VON GOETHE

In Control

We can experience joy in our
everyday lives, even when things
aren't going our way. We simply
have to remember that He is in
control. We have our being. . .
in Him!

Keep Love

Keep love in your heart. A life
without it is like a sunless garden
when the flowers are dead.
The consciousness of loving and
being loved brings a warmth and
richness to life that nothing else
can bring.

OSCAR WILDE

Press On!

A new life begins for us with every
second. Let us go forward joyously
to meet it. We must press on,
whether we will or no, and we shall
walk better with our eyes before us
than with them ever cast behind.

JEROME K. JEROME

Only Him

The Holy Spirit speaking in the
secret chambers of the heart is
the climax of God's revelation to
us. It is what gives us hope. None
but God can satisfy the longing of
the immortal soul: The heart was
made for Him. He only can fill it.

RICHARD TRENCH

Instruments

The art of life is to live in the
present moment and to make
that moment as perfect as we can
by the realization that we are the
instruments and expression of
God Himself.

EMMET FOX

Just Be

Don't get so busy that you forget
to simply be. Sometimes the best
way to stop being overwhelmed by
life is to simply step back, take a
day. . .or an hour. . .or a moment,
and notice all that God is doing in
your life.

Trust in the Lord

I waited patiently for the LORD;
he turned to me and heard my cry.
He lifted me out of the slimy pit,
out of the mud and mire; he set my
feet on a rock and gave me a firm
place to stand. He put a new song
in my mouth, a hymn of praise to
our God.

PSALM 40:1–3 NIV

Rejoice!

On earth, we may never
comprehend God's desire or plan
to save us, but through the ages,
all Christians have joined in
worship and praise of One who
gives so willingly and generously.
We can certainly rejoice in
the results, as we experience
overwhelming evidence of the
Savior's love.

Kindness Is. . .

Kindness has been described in
many ways. It is the poetry of the
heart, the music of the world.
It is a golden chain that binds
society together. It is a fountain of
gladness.

Wonder of Living

The wonder of living is held
within the beauty of silence,
the glory of sunlight, the sweetness
of fresh spring air, the quiet
strength of earth, and the love that
lies at the very root of all things.

Small Pleasures

Happiness consists more in small
conveniences or pleasures that
occur every day, than in great
pieces of good fortune that happen
but seldom to a man in the course
of his life.

BENJAMIN FRANKLIN

Sweet Savor

Your prayers certainly don't have
to be elaborate or polished. God
does not judge your way with
words. He knows your heart.
He wants to hear from you. His
Word says that your prayers rise
up to heaven like incense from the
earth. Remember to send a sweet
savor His way daily.

MARLA TIPTON

Live Carefree!

Be content with who you are, and don't put on airs. God's strong hand is on you; he'll promote you at the right time. Live carefree before God; he is most careful with you.

1 PETER 5:6–7 MSG

Extend Mercy

The more merciful we are to those
who wrong us, the more merciful
God is to us. And blessings flow out
of relationships that extend mercy.
Want to experience true joy today?
Give. . .and receive. . .mercy.

Real Love

Real love is a force more
formidable than any other.
It is invisible—it cannot be seen
or measured, yet it is powerful
enough to transform you in a
moment, and offer you more
joy than any material possession
could.

BARBARA DE ANGELIS

Joy in Friendship

Life is full of people who will
make you laugh, cry, smile until
your face hurts, and so happy that
you think you'll burst. But the
ones who leave their footprints on
your soul are the ones that keep
your life going.

NATALIE BERNOT

Beyond the Power of Words

Neglect, indifference,
forgetfulness, ignorance, are
all impossible to [God].
He knows everything; He cares
about everything; and He loves
us! Surely this is enough for a
"fullness of joy" beyond the power
of words to express.

HANNAH WHITALL SMITH

His Bounty

God wants nothing from us except
our needs, and these furnish Him
with room to display His bounty
when He supplies them freely. . . .
Not what I have, but what I do not
have, is the first point of contact
between my soul and God.

CHARLES H. SPURGEON

Glad Goodness

God is the highest good—good
as nothing else is but Himself.
He is intrinsically happy; in fact,
all good and all true happiness
are to be found only in God,
since they are essential to His
nature. No one can be happy or
experience any goodness unless
God communicates His own glad
goodness, and nothing pleases
unless it is a vehicle for God.

JOHN BUNYAN

Surprised Out of Our Socks

Hope is not a granted wish or
a favor performed; no, it is far
greater than that. It is a zany,
unpredictable dependence on God
who loves to surprise us out of our
socks.

MAX LUCADO

Garden of the Lord

Since we have so often experienced
our deserts to be turned into the
garden of the Lord, and have
found fir trees and myrtle trees
coming up where we thought there
were only thorns and briers,
the marvelous thing is that
we should ever let ourselves
be so utterly cast down and
overwhelmed when fresh trouble
comes.

HANNAH WHITALL SMITH

Perfect Love

And so we know and rely on the
love God has for us. God is love.
Whoever lives in love lives in God,
and God in him. . . . There is no
fear in love. But perfect love drives
out fear.

1 JOHN 4:16, 18 NIV

He's at Work in Me

Lord, I know that You are the One
at work in me; Your Spirit is a part
of me, and You guide my thoughts
and actions. Thank You for that.
I don't know what I would do if I
had to live life on my own.

Tomorrow's Success

Be of good cheer. Do not think of today's failure, but of the success that may come tomorrow. You . . .will find joy in overcoming obstacles. Remember, no effort that we make to attain something beautiful is ever lost.

HELEN KELLER

In His Sight

Keep a clear eye toward life's end.
Do not forget your purpose and
destiny as God's creature. What
you are in His sight is what you are
and nothing more.

ST. FRANCIS OF ASSISI

Utmost Importance

Love is of utmost importance.
Once you have set your will that
you will learn the way of love,
then there is no flaw or irritation
in another person that you cannot
bear. . . . If this one commandment
were kept—"Love one another"—
I know that it would carry us a
long way toward keeping all the
rest of our Lord's commands.

ST. TERESA OF AVILA

Good News!

Everyone has inside of him a piece
of good news. The good news is
that you don't know how great you
can be! How much you can love!
What you can accomplish!
And what your potential is!

ANNE FRANK

All Things Are Possible

All things are possible to him who
believes, more to him who hopes,
even more to him who loves, and
more still to him who practices
and perseveres in these three
virtues.

BROTHER LAWRENCE

Just Simple Joy

Today, whatever may annoy,
The word for me is Joy,
    just simple Joy.
Whate'er there be of Sorrow
I'll put off till Tomorrow,
And when Tomorrow comes,
    why then
'Twill be Today and Joy again.

JOHN KENDRICK BANGS

New Every Morning

Oh, what joy rises in our souls
as we realize that God's love and
mercy are new every morning!
Each day is a fresh start, a new
chance. Grace washes over us
afresh, like the morning dew.
Great is His faithfulness!

Hunting for Happiness

If you ever find happiness by
hunting for it, you will find it
as the old woman did her lost
spectacles, safe on her own nose
all the time.

JOSH BILLINGS

Hugs!

Everyone was meant to share
    God's all-abiding love and care;
He saw that we would
    need to know
A way to let those feelings show. . . .
So God made hugs.

JILL WOLF

For the Love of God

The most excellent method I have
of going to God is in doing my
common business without any
view of pleasing men. My hope
of glory is found in performing
purely for the love of God.

BROTHER LAWRENCE

Divine Gift

Love.
What is love?
No one can define it.
It's something so great,
   only God could design it.
Yes, love is beyond
   what man can define.
For love is immortal.
And God's gift is divine.

HELEN STEINER RICE

Be Yourself!

You simply have to be yourself—
at any age—as God made you,
available to Him so that He can
work in and through you to bring
about His kingdom and His glory.

LUCI SWINDOLL

Sweet and Pleasant

Love is a great thing, an altogether
good gift, the only thing that
makes burdens light and bears all
that is hard with ease. It carries
a weight without feeling it and
makes all that is bitter sweet and
pleasant to the taste.

THOMAS À KEMPIS

Love Is. . .

Love is patient, love is kind. It does not envy, it does not boast, it is not proud. It is not rude, it is not self-seeking, it is not easily angered, it keeps no record of wrongs. Love does not delight in evil but rejoices with the truth. It always protects, always trusts, always hopes, always perseveres.

1 CORINTHIANS 13:4–7 NIV

Excellent Things

Excellent things! God doesn't just
do good things or the best things.
He does excellent things. What
could improve on God's superb
plan or will? Are our eyes open to
the excellent things He's done for
His people—and is still doing for
them today?

Receive Joyfully

Thanksgiving puts power in living,
because it opens the generators of
the heart to respond gratefully,
to receive joyfully, and to react
creatively.

Spring Will Come

Even in the winter, even in the
midst of the storm, the sun is still
there. Somewhere, up above the
clouds, it still shines and warms
and pulls at the life buried deep
inside the brown branches and
frozen earth. The sun is there!
Spring will come! The clouds
cannot stay forever.

GLORIA GAITHER

Seeds of Kindness

When seeds of kindness are sown
prayerfully in the garden plot
of our lives, we may be sure that
there will be a bountiful harvest of
blessings for both us and others.

W. Phillip Keller

Grace and Truth

And the Word was made flesh,
and dwelt among us, (and we
beheld his glory, the glory as of
the only begotten of the Father,)
full of grace and truth.

JOHN 1:14 KJV

Two Requirements

There are two requirements
for our proper enjoyment of
every earthly blessing which
God bestows on us—a thankful
reflection on the goodness of the
Giver and a deep sense of the
unworthiness of the receiver.
The first would make us grateful,
the second humble.

HANNAH MORE

Love Is That. . .

Love is not getting, but giving. . . .
It is goodness and honor and peace
and pure living—yes, love is that,
and it is the best thing in the world
and the thing that lives the longest.

HENRY VAN DYKE

Completely, Thoroughly, Perfectly

Grace means God accepts
me just as I am. He does not
require or insist that I measure
up to someone else's standard
of performance. He loves me
completely, thoroughly, and
perfectly. There's nothing I can do
to add or detract from that love.

MARY GRAHAM

Happy Childhood

Indeed, now that I come to
think of it, I never really feel
grown-up at all. Perhaps this is
because childhood, catching our
imagination when it is fresh and
tender, never lets go of us.

J. B. PRIESTLEY

He Will Deliver

Nothing is impossible with our
Lord! If you're in a dark place
today, call out to Him. . .and
watch as He delivers you. He will
establish your steps. Praise Him!

In His Hand

I love to think that God appoints
My portion day by day;
Events of life are in His hand,
And I would only say,
Appoint them in
  Thine own good time,
And in Thine own best way.

A. L. WARING

Incomparable Love and Joy

Occasionally I must remind
myself that all gifts are given to
me, God's beloved child, with
incomparable love and joy. . . .
Everything good and loving in life
has its source in God, including
all gifts.

MARILYN MEBERG

Learning Love

Is life not full of opportunities for learning love? Every man and woman every day has a thousand of them. The world is not a playground; it is a schoolroom. Life is not a holiday, but an education. And the one eternal lesson for us all is how better we can love.

HENRY DRUMMOND

Everywhere Present

God. . .is everywhere present.
He is not an occasional visitor,
nor ever more truly present than
at this very moment. He is always
ready to flow into our heart;
indeed He is there now.

ARTHUR FOOTE

Our Potential

God created us with an
overwhelming desire to soar. . . .
He designed us to be tremendously
productive and "to mount up with
wings like eagles," realistically
dreaming of what He can do with
our potential.

CAROL KENT

The Way Home

Thank You for Your promise
to guide me in all things great
and small. Your eye is always on
me, keeping me from error and
ensuring that I can always find a
way home to You.

His Love, Like Sunshine

May God send His love like
 sunshine in His warm and
 gentle way,
To fill each corner of your heart
 each moment of today.

Manna

Happiness is like manna;
it is to be gathered in grains,
and enjoyed every day. It will not
keep; it cannot be accumulated;
nor have we got to go out of
ourselves or into remote places to
gather it, since it is rained down
from heaven, at our very doors.

TRYON EDWARDS

This Is Christmas

This is Christmas: not the tinsel,
not the giving and receiving,
not even the carols, but the
humble heart that receives anew
the wondrous gift, the Christ.

FRANK MCKIBBEN

Magic of Christmas

The joy of brightening other lives,
bearing others' burdens, easing
others' loads and supplanting
empty hearts and lives with
generous gifts becomes for us the
magic of Christmas.

W. C. JONES

His Children

But when the right time came,
God sent his Son, born of a
woman, subject to the law.
God sent him to buy freedom for
us who were slaves to the law, so
that he could adopt us as his very
own children.

GALATIANS 4:4–5 NLT

The Dawn of Morning

Conversions are like the dawn of morning: They come and eradicate the very dewdrops and change them to jewels; they wake all the birds; they wake all the hearts and melodies.

PHILLIPS BROOKS

Joy Comes Back

For somehow, not only at
　　Christmas,
But all the long year through,
The joy that you give to others,
Is the joy that comes back to you.

JOHN GREENLEAF WHITTIER

New Beginnings

Today, ponder the new beginnings
in your own life. Hasn't God
recreated you? Renewed you?
Won't He do the same for others?
Feel the joy rise up as you ponder
the possibilities!

Everywhere Christmas

Everywhere, everywhere,
Christmas tonight!
Christmas in the lands of
the fir tree and pine,
Christmas in the lands of
the palm tree and vine,
Christmas where snow peaks
stand solemn and white.
Christmas where cornfields
stand sunny and bright. . . .

PHILLIPS BROOKS

Sing in Exultation!

Sing, choirs of angels,
  sing in exultation!
O sing, all ye citizens
  of heav'n above;
Glory to God, glory in the highest.
O come, let us adore Him.
O come, let us adore Him,
O come, let us adore Him,
  Christ the Lord.

JOHN FRANCIS WADE

God Is Everywhere

It is surprising how easy it is to hear music in the waves and songs in the wild whisperings of the winds; to see God everywhere in the stones, in the rocks, in the rippling brooks, and hear Him everywhere, in the lowing of cattle, in the rolling of thunder, and in the fury of tempests.

CHARLES H. SPURGEON

Time Management

Effective time management means having time left over to do the things you want to do. It gives you time to spend with family and friends, to be creative and enjoy life.

LEE SILBER

The First Consciousness of Love

There is nothing holier,
  in this life of ours,
Than the first consciousness
  of love,
The first fluttering of
  its silken wings—
The first rising sound and breath
  of that wind which is
So soon to sweep thru the soul.

HENRY WADSWORTH LONGFELLOW

Now!

What we need is not new light, but
new sight; not new paths, but new
strength to walk in the old ones;
not new duties, but new wisdom
from on high to fulfill those that
are plain before us.

Life and Breath

"Which of all these does not know
that the hand of the LORD has
done this? In his hand is the life
of every creature and the breath of
all mankind."

JOB 12:9–10 NIV

Scripture Index

OLD TESTAMENT

NEW TESTAMENT